MY PLEA FOR YOU

BY

BENITA NICHOLS

OTHER BOOKS BY BENITA NICHOLS

HAROLD AND COMPANY parts 1 thru 4
HAROLD AND THE STALKERS and other plays
THE WALLFLOWERS
RIVALRY IN THE ROMPER ROOM
TERESA AND THE DOCTOR
WE ARE FAMILY
THE SQUARE PEG
THE FLIP SIDE parts 1 thru 9
DISCO SUPERSTAR
FAITH OF THE RAGDOLL
RAGS TO RICHES parts 1 thru 6
GOOD TRIUMPHS OVER EVIL
A BRIDE FOR HUMPERDINCK
SOUTHERN STYLE HUMPERDINCK and other plays
SAPPHIRE
THE LITTLE MAN IN THE BIG SHOES
LAUGHTER THROUGH THE SEASONS
ADVENTURES WITH FRIENDS OLD AND NEW
MEETING MY FRIENDS AT THE WISHING WELL
GOLDEN NUGGETS AT THE END OF THE RAINBOW
STAIRWAY TO THE STARS
SEEDS OF DREAMS
DANCING IN THE RAIN
MY BOOK OF CHRISTMAS POEMS
GOD WHISPERS TO MY HEART
A GARDEN FILLED WITH PRAISES
PRAYERS FROM THE HEART
and others

Orders of these books can be purchased at Amazon.com.

This book is dedicated to Almighty God who is the Creator of earth and heaven, and my husband, Bernard, who encourages me to write.

MY PLEA FOR YOU

My precious friend, when I suffered,
Bleeding on the cross I was nailed upon,
Tears blurred my eyes while I prayed for you
As the gravity of sin weighed me down.

I took your punishment, for I loved you so dearly
That I would shatter Hell's gates and crush Satan's head
So you would never suffer as did I--
My plan for you-- the Promised Land to keep you well-fed.

Precious friend, lay all of your guilt at my feet,
Then turn away from your sins and run to my face--
I love you, you are forgiven, and I will keep you
Cradled in the blessings of my love, my mercy, and my
grace.

PRAY WITHOUT CEASING

Keep watch and pray without ceasing,
Satan is a liar and will never stop deceiving,
Even attempting to blindside God's children,
But by the blood of the Lamb, victory you will win.
Darker and darker is becoming the night,
But never will darkness overpower the light,
Jesus has already fought and won the battle for you,
Pray without ceasing-- soon is coming a breakthrough.

HOLDING YOUR HAND

My child, I am holding your hand
As you stumble in a troubled land,
Do not fear,
I am always here
Guiding and leading you
With my love and truth.
Trust my hand
In a dark land.

TRUST MY WORD

Be not afraid but trust My Word
As you watch and pray,
And I will guide your feet
All of the way.
I will protect you
All through the night,
Holding your hand
While leading you with My light.

PROTECTION

My Savior, let the little ones know
They will be protected in Your love,
And no one can do them any harm
As You watch them from above.

STRONG WIND

My precious little one, the wind may be strong
As the storm lasts too long,
But I'm keeping you safe inside My wing
Whispering peace to you while I sing
To comfort your trembling soul--
My love heals and makes you whole.
My precious little one, this, please understand--
No strong wind will blow you from My hand.

LIGHT IN MY HEART

Inside my heart is a light
Shining and burning bright
While darkness surrounds me
But not completely;
Holy is the fire,
Growing is my desire
To continue to pray
And follow Jesus all the way.

MOLD MY HEART

Mold my heart, Lord, and shape it according to Your will
As You stand by my side, speaking in a voice soft and still;
Search my heart, Lord, for hidden sins, lead me by Your
love and light,
And teach me, my dear Lord, to live right.

PLEA FOR MY PEOPLE

My people, who are called by My Name,
Turn from what brings shame
To Me, and repent of all of your sin--
Then you will watch Me heal the land from within.

SOON I AM RETURNING

I am the Beginning and the End,
I loved you so much, with My blood
I cleared your sins and gave you life.
Salvation is in My hand,
You are saved by My grace,
And soon I am returning to end all strife.
My people, there are ways that seem right,
But there is only one way,
And that way is through Me.
Trust not the words of men,
But My Word, the double-edged sword
Which cuts through the soul and sets you free.

MY LONGING FOR YOU

My children, turn your hearts toward Me,
For I love you and offer you My grace.
My heart was broken and I spilled My blood
To deliver you from a horrible place.
I am grieved when you refuse to obey,
And feel the agony as I was nailed to the cross.
How I long to gather you in My arms--
I never want you to be lost.
I am willing to bless you beyond your dreams,
Give you abundant life never to end,
Heal and deliver you completely--
Come to Me-- so many blessings I will send.

I SURRENDER MY HEART TO YOU

My dear Lord, I surrender to You my heart for You to
search with Your light,
If any uncleanness resides in me, purify my heart and make
me right,
Measure my motives by Your standards of holy love
And keep me focused on You above.

I WILL DELIVER YOU

My dear friend, your suffering will not last long,
I am with you comforting you with My song
To help you become strong.
Soon I will deliver you from the binding chain,
Show you the blessings gained,
And you will run freely again.

I AM ON MY WAY

My child, again turn toward My face.
Remember My mercy and grace
When I rescued you from sin
And healed you from deep within?
We would fellowship in love,
You would look above
And hold on to My truth
That helped you through.
You awaited my return,
Your love for Me burned.
Even though it seems I delayed,
Still, I am on My way.
I will arrive as a thief in the night--
Be sure you are living right.

CONVICT MY HEART

My Lord, remind me how much I need You
And convict my heart to hold on to Your truth,
Help me to grow in Your love and grace
And embrace all of Your ways.

HOLY AND BLESSED

My Lord, my God, You created everything;
My Lord, my God, all the creatures sing
Of Your glory; You are holy, blessed is Your Name;
My Lord, my God, You remain the same!

HOW AWESOME IS HE

How awesome is our Lord on His throne!
All of the elders cast before Him their crowns,
Glory and honor they bring
While praising His holy Name as they sing!

THE LAMB GAVE HIS LIFE

The Lamb sacrificed His life and rose alive again
As the Victor over death-- He paid the penalty for sin
And set all of the captives free to forever live;
He is the Lion of Judah-- glory and honor He gives.

THANK YOU FOR LOVING ME

Thank You, Jesus, for loving me so much
That You looked beyond my sins and saw my tortured soul,
Then imparted to me forgiveness,
Healing me, delivering me, and making me whole.

MY PROMISE

My faithful servant, I have heard your prayers and seen
your good works;
Soon I am coming to gather you in My arms and love away
everything that hurts;
Trust My hand regardless of what happens around you, and
continue to obey;
Never will I fail, just hold onto My truth-- still, I will return
on the appointed Day.

LEAD ME ON YOUR NARROW WAY

Holy Spirit, steady my feet on Your narrow way,
Convict my heart as I pray,
And guide me in Your peace and love
As I keep looking above.

GUIDE THEM, MY LORD

My Lord, my God, for those who are ill,
Reach out, touch, and heal;
For the ones shivering in fear,
May they know You are standing near;
For the ones deep in sorrow,
Show them a bright tomorrow;
For the ones who have lost their way,
Bring them to an endless day;
For the ones hardened and cold,
Reveal to them You are worth more than gold;
For the ones blinded by sin,
Show them Your light so they can come in;
For those confused, knowing not what to do,
Let them know Your Word is true.

RESTORATION

Your holy Father listens when you pray
And will bring forth a new day
When He will take away all pain
And reveal all of your blessings gained;
He will dry all of your tears
And restore all of the lost years.

TO LOVE YOU MORE

Jesus, I wish everyone would love You the way I do,
Praying, singing You praises, and living Your truth;
You stretched wide Your arms on the cross and sacrificed
Your life for my sin,
Giving me love, peace, and joy while delivering and
healing me deep within.

Jesus, I wish everyone would love You more than I do,
I took a good look at myself-- I cannot compare myself to
You,
All of my righteousness burns to ashes in the fire You test
me through,
Help me to love what You love and hold on to Your truth.

JESUS WILL ALWAYS LOVE YOU

Jesus, will always love you,
He longs for you to live in His truth,
He gave His life on the cross
So you would have no reason to be lost,
He will fill you with mercy and grace
When you come to Him in faith.

LIVING SEED

I have placed seed in your hand
To be cast upon My holy ground,
You need not care where the seed lands--
I foresee where it is bound
As My sun and rain help it take root
And branch out east, west, north, and south,
Becoming a harvest of finest fruit
Sweet and tasty in the mouth.
When the ground is hard and dry,
My wind blows it away
Or birds take it as they fly in the sky
To give the seed a new place to stay.
My seed lives and produces a harvest
Stretching far and wide,
My seed is My Word that will bless
All around, inside, and outside.

JESUS IS COMING SOON

Jesus is coming soon,
Maybe morning, midnight, or noon
To take us to the Promised Land--
Solid rock, not sinking sand.

I LONG TO OPEN MY HEART

My dear loved one, I long to open my heart and share
With overflowing tender care
My deep love for you
As I reach out to help you through
The troubles and struggles we face today.
I long to open my heart to pray.

THE LOVE OF JESUS

Only the love of Jesus
Can pierce through a hardened heart
And soften it as clay
And shine light where it is dark.
Only the love of Jesus
Can wash away the stan of sin
And clean every blemish
Deep within.

LONGING TO LOVE AS YOU LOVE

Jesus, I long to love as You do--
Sacrificial, holy, and giving, too;
Guide my steps along Your narrow way,
Fill me daily with faith as I pray,
Take all selfish gain away from me,
And humble me-- Jesus, You get the glory.
It doesn't matter if I'm not well received,
What matters most is that I'm not deceived
Into thinking the works are my own--
Jesus, what I have, to You these works belong.
Jesus, I long to love as You do--
Sharing peace and joy from a heart faithful and true.
Jesus, blow the chaff from me with the wind
And fill my heart with love so I won't sin.

FILL ME WITH FRESH FIRE

Holy Spirit, feel me with fresh fire
And renew me with desire
To press on when I am weary
And to seek joy from You when my eyes are teary.

THANK YOU FOR BLESSING ME

Thank You, Father, for one more day
And answering me when I pray;
Thank You, for the peace You bring
And for giving me a voice to sing
Praises for the blessings You supply,
Blessings that continue to multiply.
Thank You, Father, for joy and love
That I will never get enough of.

MAKE ME FRUITFUL

My Lord, help me to be a faithful servant
Who tills the land You placed in my hand
And casts seed upon the ground
For a harvest of fruit throughout the land.

A SEED OF LOVE

If you plant a seed of love into God's good ground,
It will take root and grow into a joyful tree, solid and
sound.
The tree will produce succulent fruit, nourishing to the
soul,
And all who eat the fruit will be healed and made whole.

YOUR BATTLE HAS BEEN WON

Satan has no power over you,
The blood of the Lamb has set you free;
Whatever weapon used against you,
Your Savior fights your battle and wins the victory.

Your Savior nailed all your sins at the cross,
Then rose from death and crushed Satan's head;
Never give up-- whatever is gained will not be lost--
Jesus has won the battle with His blood, alive and red.

JESUS STANDS NEARBY

Jesus stands nearby
Listening to your heart's cry,
Willingly offering His hand
To help you to stand
In your moment of weakness;
He will give you rest.

TO LIVE FOR JESUS

Jesus, I love You with my whole heart,
Forsaking what the world has to give;
I'm dying to pride and seeking Your will,
For You, Jesus, I want to live.

THE POWER OF WORDS

My Lord, move Your Spirit within me to speak words
Which will build a bridge but not tear down a house,
Calm a storm but not damage a field of crops,
Knock down a stone wall but not harm a mouse,
Strengthen the weak but not trip the crippled,
Heal the sick but not inflict pain;
Help me to realize life and death are in words--
They can cause loss or bring gain.

JESUS IS THE ONLY WAY

Jesus has opened the door of His lighthouse for you to enter
in
To step out of the darkness of sin,
The light of His lamp burns night and day--
He is the only way.
Jesus freely gives you mercy and grace,
His love can never be replaced
With whatever this world has to give--
Come to Jesus and truly live.

HELP ME TO LOVE

Holy Father, help me to love and pray
Everyday,
And fill my heart with joy and peace to give
As long as I live.

ADORATION

Lord God Almighty, holy is Your Name,
Your glory remains the same,
You are faithful and true,
With all of my heart I love and honor You,
Praises to You I sing,
My soon coming Lord and King!

MY BIG STRONG LOVE

Trust Me, My child, My love is big enough to swallow
All of your sorrow
And replace it with laughter in My light.

My love will dry all of your tears
And chase away all of your fears;
I will turn your rainy days sunshine bright.

My love is strong
And lasts eternally long;
I will restore what has been stolen from you.

From your heart you have been faithfully giving
And you will receive My blessings in the land of the living
As My promises shine through.

KEEP LISTENING, KEEP WATCHING

Keep listening, keep watching,
For the holy Lord Almighty will come as a thief in the
night;
Keep praying, keep obeying,
Keep putting oil in your lamp to keep it burning bright;
Look not at the stormy waves of the sea,
Turn your eyes to your Savior's face;
Listen not to what other voices tell you to do,
Lend your ears to Jesus' words of mercy and grace;
Keep in mind that He is coming soon,
And this troubled world will pass away;
Keep listening, keep watching,
Keep being willing to yield and pray.

HELP ME KEEP THE FAITH

Jesus, help me to keep the faith
As I seek Your face and pray,
Show me Your path shining bright
With Your love and holy light.

MY HEART BELONGS TO YOU

My heart belongs to You, Jesus,
My Savior, Lord, and King;
All I have is Yours, Jesus,
You are my everything!

I LONG TO TOUCH YOUR HEART

Father, how I love holding Your hand
While journeying through this turbulent land
With storm clouds darkening the sky.
Sometimes it seems You are faraway; always You are
nearby.
I sing You praises for blessing me,
Guiding me along the way, and providing light to see
By pointing out the brightest star.
Father, I long to be so close to You that I can touch Your
heart.

WHERE WILL YOU BE?

Today wrong is seen as good and right is put to shame
While evildoers disobey God and dishonor His Name.
They stick their fingers in their ears, ignoring when the
Lord is calling,
Leading many astray-- all around so many are falling;
But the time is coming when Almighty God will judge sin--
Where will you be when judgement begins?

PRAISE TO MY KING

My Savior Jesus, my King, my everything,
I give You high praises and sing
Glory to Your Name for Your mercy and grace
As I honor all of Your ways!
You are faithful and true
And there is none like You!
I will lift my voice
And sing You rejoice!

NO FORCE STRONG ENOUGH

No force is so strong
It can overthrow my Savior's power;
He is my love and light,
My high tower!

WHAT IS GOING ON?

My Lord, I look around myself and don't like what I see--
People are being as bad as they can be!
Rioting, fighting, destroying, burning buildings down,
Shooting, looting, defacing-- destruction is all around!
What is going on? I've never seen it this bad;
I know it disgusts You-- it makes me sad.
Why do they want to steal? Why do they want to kill?
Don't they realize if they pray, this land you will heal?
Why won't they reach out to You so they can see Your
truth?
They are blind and have lost their minds and are doing
what sinners do.
My Lord, please speak to their hearts before everything is
shattered;
Let them know You are Lord of all and all lives matter.

YOUR PRESENCE

Your presence, Holy Spirit, calms me
As the cool breeze when I walk
In the early summer morn.
A bluebird sings in the magnolia tree
A melody of Your presence,
Sweet, loving, and warm.
Your presence, Holy Spirit, soothes me
When turmoil is all around;
Your presence keeps me calm.

THERE IS COMING A DAY

There is coming a day
When the last teardrop is wiped away;
Coming tomorrow
Is the end of sorrow.
Joy and peace will not walk on by,
We will enjoy the fruit of answered prayers--
No more worries, no more cares.
There is coming a day
When sin will be blown away.

I WANT TO BE CLOSE TO YOU

I want to be so close to You, my Lord,
That I am tightly hugging Your heart;
I want to love You so sincerely
That all strife is drained out of me,
And Your joy and peace settles in,
Leaving no room for sin.
My Lord, I want to love You so dearly
That my eyes open wide and see clearly
Any device Satan may use
To blindside, deceive, or confuse.
Guide me as I read Your Word and pray;
Hold my hand as I walk Your narrow way.

AN AMAZING CITY

Coming is an amazing city with beauty that will blind the
eye,
A city where joy is never-ending, peace is everlasting, and
there is no need to cry
Because disease and death have been destroyed; no longer
does day become night.
The glory of God and the Lamb will be the source of the
light!

SEEKING YOU

Day by day I seek Your face,
You fill me with Your saving grace,
Your love falls upon me like sunshine,
And peace leads me time after time;
Thank You, my Lord, for always being there
Guiding my feet and answering prayer.

HE IS COMING SOON

He is coming soon!
Jesus is coming soon!
No more death! No more doom!
We will be welcome to His living water
And will eat from the Tree of Life!
Jesus nailed all of our sins at the cross
And rose from the grave to life!

KEEP YOUR FIRE ALIVE

My Lord, keep Your fire alive in my soul,
Let it burn away the chaff, heal me, and make me whole,
My Lord, let Your fire reveal pure gold
When I stand before Your glory-- let my passion not grow
cold.

NO TURNING BACK

There is no turning back from my Savior's love,
He is my solid rock below and my protection from above;
No wind will blow my faith away
Because I stand my ground and pray.

LEAD ME

Lead me, Holy Spirit, along Your narrow way
As I seek Your truth, and guide me as I pray;
Show me where to go and what to do--
Holy Spirit, I want to be led by You.

GODLY GIFTS

My Lord, no earthly treasure
By no means can measure
To the gifts You give,
Blessings that live,
Producing fruit in the harvest
With seed which is the best.

FALLING ON WEAKENED KNEES

My Lord, my God, humbly I fall before Your altar on
weakened knees
Beseeching You to help me to live my life for Your love
and peace.
I cannot do this on my own because I am of flesh, but Your
Spirit lives in me as my Guide.
My Lord, my God, burn Your Word in my heart to keep me
on Your narrow path and to help me not to surrender to
pride.

PROMOTION

Persecution may come from the deeds of people,
But promotion is given from God's hand;
No matter how high the pressure, obey and wait on the
Lord
Who willingly gives you the strength to stand.

JESUS, I LOVE YOU

To You, Jesus, I long to draw nearer,
Your way, I long to see clearer,
My heart, I want to grow dearer
As I seek You day by day,,
As I worship You and pray,
As I follow Your narrow way;
How much I love Your truth,
How I admire what You do,
Jesus, I love You.

NONE LIKE YOU

My Lord, there is none like You,
There is no other truth,
Yours is the only way,
To You I pray.

PRAISES

My Lord, I choose to walk in Your ways
All of my days,
Giving You glory, and singing You praise--
My voice I raise!

TOUCH WHAT HURTS

Holy Spirit, I need Your healing power
This very hour;
Touch what hurts and take away the pain
In Your healing rain.

THE TRUE HEALER

Time is a healer, I often hear,
But days, weeks, months, even a year
Does not wipe away one tear.
Pain often cuts so deep
It piles sorrow too steep
For the fastest antelope to leap.
But the hands of Jesus will heal
All kinds of wounds and fill
Emptiness with His love, so real.
He gives perfect joy and peace,
He meets all kinds of needs,
The deepest pain, He will ease.

PRAYING FOR YOU

I take your pain to heart
As I go to the Lord
Praying for you;
My Lord will pull you through.

COME INTO THIS PLACE

Holy Spirit, come into this place
With Your power and healing ways,
Touch all who are feeling helpless,
Reach out, Holy Spirit, and bless.

WEAR THE WHOLE ARMOR

Spiritual wickedness wait in high places to swoop down
upon us in moments of weakness.
We need the whole armor of God to stand against the wiles
of the devil; it is not flesh
And blood we are wrestling against-- it is the power of
darkness tempting us to sin.
Be prepared with the whole armor for complete protection
to keep from giving in.

I FIGHT YOUR BATTLES

Allow Me to fight your battles
When the Enemy rushes in like a storm,
For you are of flesh and blood
And will cause only harm.
You are ill-equipped to handle evil--
You need My Spirit for strength;
I battle demons with a strong arm
Of never-ending length.
Demons cringe and cower
At My mighty hand--
Trust in the faith I give you
To hold on and stand.

PROTECTED IN MY HAND

I am the calm eye of the storm
Protecting you from all harm,
No matter how the wind bends the trees,
The storm ceases when I speak peace;
I hear your heart's silent prayer,
You are safe in my care,
No storm will blow you down--
You are in My hand, safe and sound.

LISTEN, WATCH, AND WAIT

Listen, watch, and wait;
Get ready before it is too late.
Jesus is coming soon,
Maybe midnight or afternoon.
Step out of darkness and into the light,
Get washed in the blood and start living right,
The world as we know it is wearing out,
Start believing and stop giving in to doubt.
Remember way back in Noah's days?
People refused to walk in God's ways,
God locked the door of the ark, the rain fell down,
And all those people drowned.
Listen, watch, and wait;
Soon it will be too late
When Jesus comes through the open sky--
If you are not ready, you will cry.

PRAYING FOR YOUR HEALING

Tonight I pray healing for you
And that all of your hopes shine through
Like sunrise reflected on a lake;
May you receive all promises Jesus makes.

JOY

Jesus brings joy that overshadows sorrow
And sends a glorious tomorrow
With answered prayers
Everywhere!

ANSWERED PRAYER

Thank You, Jesus, for answering my prayer
When I was in dire need of tender loving care;
You healed my lonely, broken life
And transformed me into a happy wife.

GOD'S LOVE IS REAL

God's love is so real
That it will mend and heal
Whatever has been broken;
His will is done as His Word is spoken.

ETERNITY IS COMING

A barrage of problems is plaguing the world today,
Someone needs to do something, I hear people say;
Yes, this is so true,
But what can we do?
Have patience, keep the faith, and pray;
Jesus will soon be on His way,
Splitting wide the sky
To bring us home on high.
A barrage of problems will soon be left behind;
There will be eternity and no more time.

JESUS ON THE WING

Jesus is waiting on the wing
To settle everything,
Step out of darkness and into the light,
Stop doing wrong and start living right.

WILLING TO SERVE

My Lord, I am willing to serve You
With an open heart, faithful and true,
Keeping my eyes on You above
As I travel Your road of love.

GREAT WEALTH

In God's kingdom is a great wealth
Of blessings that restore joy and health,
Blessings bringing peace and love
With faith always rising above.

OUR LOVING FATHER

Our Father is not heavy-handed toward the ones He loves;
He is compassionate, assuring they will be taken care of,
Protecting and shielding them from what will cause harm.
We can trust our Father who keeps us in His arms.

JESUS IS ON YOUR SIDE

I may not be there,
But I hold you in my heart in prayer
For your healing to arrive--
Jesus is on your side.

PRAYER FOR MY LOVED ONES

My Lord, I come to You, my heart heavily filled with deep
prayer,
Asking You to touch the hearts of my dear loved ones and
let them know I care
When their tiresome loads are bearing them down with
sorrow.
I long to be by their sides when they are feeling tired and
low.
Miles separate, but love binds us together-- yes-- I will
continue to love.
My Lord, help them to look not at the choppy waves of the
stormy sea below, but toward Your bright face above.

YOUR HEALER HAS ARRIVED

Your Healer has arrived in this place,
His heart is overflowing with mercy and grace
As He stretches His hands over everything sore,
Touching and blessing until your health is restored.

HEALING AND DELIVERY

I feel Your warmth on my face
Like summer sunshine all over the place,
You are healing and delivering today,
Answering every prayer I pray!

PRAYER FOR DELIVERANCE

My Lord, I pray for eyes to open toward Your light,
Ears to hear Your voice in the silence of night,
And hearts to receive Your hands that touch and feel
Deep wounds which You will heal.
Deliver the ones trapped in Satan's snares
So they will receive answers to their desperate prayers.

BIND US IN LOVE

My Father, release us from strongholds and bind us
together with Your ribbons of love,
Unshackle our hands so we will readily and willingly give
to those in need,
Touch our hearts with Your mercy and grace as You make
our hearts as pliable as clay,
And, most of all, my Father, convict us to throw away
pride; humble us as we pray.

COME TO ME

I am your Savior ready and willing to bless
You with My everlasting peace when you are stressed
By the heavy load you have to bear--
Just come to Me in prayer.

THANK YOU FOR BLESSING US

Thank You, Father, for blessing us today
For a time to praise You and pray
As You steady our feet on Your path of love
While watching us from above.

THANK YOU FOR GUIDING ME

Father, I thank You for guiding me on Your path of love
As I venture into Your vineyard to serve You
With a devoted heart. Continue to lead me with Your eye
As I seek Your truth.

MY SAVIOR HEARS ME

I long to comfort you, but you have turned away,
So I will go to the bosom of my Savior and pray
For you to receive the peace you need.
My Savior hears me-- your soul He will feed.

WE ARE HEALED AND DELIVERED

Yes, my Lord , my God, my Father in heaven, Your hands
heal, and You deliver us from the deceiver and spring us
from his snares.
The Blood of the Lamb covers us, the Holy Ghost seals us
from the destroyer, and You hear and answer all of our
prayers.
Our adversary, the devil, as a roaring lion, walks about
seeking whom he may devour, but our Savior, Jesus, the
Lion of Judah, rose from death and crushed the devil's head
to free us from sin.
By His stripes we are healed, by His blood we are
delivered, and heaven's doors are open to let us in.

COVERED AND HEALED

Jesus, thank You for never leaving my side,
In You I always abide
Because You covered all of my sins
And healed me from deep within.

HE IS RUSHING TO YOUR DEFENSE

Trust Jesus when life no longer makes sense;
He will rush to your defense,
Willing to heal and deliver you
As He arrives to your rescue.

GUIDE ME IN MY WALKS

My precious Lord, as I walk along Your pathway of love today,
Cover my heart with Your peace so I will not stray
When I come across a bend where I cannot see.
Guide my spirit and show it is faith, not sight, leading me.

THE PRESENCE OF THE HOLY SPIRIT

The presence of the Holy Spirit is here
Casting away every fear
And replacing it with peace
That calms troubled seas.
The Holy Spirit is touching all over the place,
Healing and delivering with mercy and grace.
The Holy Spirit has given comfort to you
With complete peace and power of truth.

ROCK-SOLID TRUTH

My Holy God, in Your eyes no matter is too small,
And no order, my precious Lord, is too tall.
I come before You praising You for all You do
And thanking You for Your rock-solid truth.
I pray You reach out to comfort and heal--
Yes, I do believe You answer prayer in Your still,
Quiet voice of a silent night
In which You shine as bright light.

GOD'S GRACE IS EVERYWHERE

Troubles may seem to appear in thin air,
But God's grace is everywhere,
Delivering you from terror by night
And the arrow that flies in daylight.
The Lord is your refuge from harm;
He will save you from a plague and protect you from a
storm.

JESUS IS PLEADING

Jesus is standing at your heart's door pleading for you to
allow Him to send
Away all of your tormentors to a wilderness with no end.
His arms are open to receive you, comfort you, and take
away your pain
While healing your past, leading you to a bright future, and
pouring out all of the rain.
Be careful not to turn away His messenger whose path you
have crossed today;
This may be the one with a word of hope, an answer to
what you did pray.

ON THE BATTLEFIELD

My precious child, hold on to faith
When it seems I'm not there,
I'm on the battlefield for you
To answer your prayer.
I meant what I promised
When I told you I would never leave,
I'm on the battlefield for you,
Continue to believe.

HE IS WILLING TO HEAL

My God Almighty is willing to heal
And bring restoration
Not only to the individual
But to the entire nation.
We must be willing to repent
And turn from our wicked ways;
My God Almighty will heal the land
If those called by His Name will pray.

TOUCH PEOPLE EVERYWHERE

My Lord, my God, hear my humble prayer
And touch people everywhere
With Your pure love and shine Your light
So all hatred will take a flight.

HEALING POWER

My Lord, I need You this very hour
To bring forth Your healing power,
Since I was a child I believed
In Your complete and perfect peace
That casts all anxiety away--
You listen to me when I pray.
Thank You, my Lord, for the strength You give
For me to prosper and live.

HIS PRESENCE IN MY HOME

I feel my Savior's presence in my home tonight
Binding my dear loved ones and making all things right,
Jesus is hearing my heart pray
And replacing fear with faith
As He comforts and soothes all the pain
With love and peace from healing rain.

HOLDING ON TO FAITH

Thank You, Jesus, for all of Your care
As You consider me and answer my prayer
While I hold on to faith,
Believing in Your awesome ways.

THE HOLY SPIRIT IS HERE

The Holy Spirit moves in this room
Healing and sending peace
To everyone here;
He is meeting all of our needs.

YOUR CLEAR VOICE

My Lord, Your voice, soft and still, rings clear,
Even in the midst of noise, and is dear to my ear;
My heart is open to obey Your truth
As are my feet to follow You.

I AM ALWAYS WITH YOU

You are never alone, for I am with you,
Guiding you with My eye, leading you by My truth;
When your pathway becomes dark, My light
Will shine all through the night sunlight bright.

WHAT I HAVE DONE FOR YOU

You need not be burdened down
When I traded the cross you were carrying with My royal
crown.
I took the nails meant for you
And had them to pierce My hands and feet all the way
through.
I even purchased your soul with My blood so you will live.
Can you even imagine all I am willing to give?

YOU ARE NEAR ME

Jesus, I feel You near me calming my fears
As You comfort me and wipe away my tears;
You keep Your promise to remain with me
Always, providing for me through all eternity.

ALWAYS IN MY CARE

My child, I have heard your prayer
And you will always be in My care;
My peace I will send--
I will never abandon you to the wind.

THE SPIRIT OF THE LORD IS HERE

The Spirit of the Lord is moving in this place
Healing, delivering, and restoring with mercy and grace;
The Spirit of the Lord brings faith and peace
To release all burdens and give sweet relief.

I WILL SHINE HIS LIGHT

God gave me His light,
I will shine it everywhere I go,
I will shine it so bright
All around, high, and low.

I DESERVE NOTHING

My dear Jesus, too many times I bring You my requests,
But I fail to thank You, and still You bless.
Jesus, thank You for giving so generously to me always--
I deserve nothing. Thank You, Jesus, for Your mercy and
grace.

MAKE MY HEART MORE LIKE YOURS

My precious Jesus, make my heart more like Yours,
Willing to love, quick to forgive, and always caring
As I pray and reach our to those in need--
Provide me a heart for giving and sharing.

LET NOT MY LIVING BE IN VAIN

Jesus, touch my heart and fill me with Your love for my
neighbor,
And bless my hands with Your peace as I go into Your
vineyard to labor;
Let not my living be in vain, but to give all honor and glory
to You,
And fill me with the joy of the Holy Spirit as I walk in Your
truth.

SURROUND ME

Surround me, Holy Spirit, with love for everyone
As I journey the pathway of peace until my days on earth
are done,
Surround me with comfort for those hurting and grieving
And guide me to help with all they are needing.

LIGHT AND LOVE

Jesus, Your light
Shines noonday bright
Even at midnight,
Your love fills
Open wounds and heals
Broken hearts and seals
Souls with peace
And feeds
All needs.

WHAT PRAYER CAN DO

Prayer reaches where fingers cannot go
And untangles bondage so love will flow
Freely so joy and peace
Will be released.

RESTORED TO HEALTH

His healing love took away all of my pain
And strengthened me so I could run again,
I was stricken by the arrows of the wicked flying in the air
And fell to the ground, then landed in the devil's snare,
But Jesus came to my rescue with His saving grace,
Picked me up, and restored my faith,
Now I am free, flying high with my restored wings;
I have joy and peace, and my spirit sings.

BE NOT DECEIVED

My dear friend, I love you and don't want you to be
deceived,
I want you to hear and listen to truth-- please believe,
There is a great lie from Satan to lead you away from God's
light--
He is telling you good is wrong and evil is right
And making a mockery of righteousness--
Literally stirring up a hornet's nest.
My friend, turn away from this darkness and live in the
light;
God loves you and wants you to live right.

MY BURDEN IN YOUR HANDS

My Lord, my heart is troubled, so I come to You
Placing my burdens in Your hands, for You are more
capable than me
To carry them and see me through.
Thank You, my Lord, for Your help. I give You all the
glory.

DARKNESS IN THE LAND

I love You, Jesus, with every ounce of strength within me,
When darkness covers the land at night, Your eyes see
What my mind is unable to discern;
I trust even now the lesson You want me to learn.

WILLING TO GIVE

I am the Savior Who sacrificed His life for you
To live abundantly in My Name and truth;
Freely I am willing to give you the best,
I will heal and restore you and provide you rest.

HELP ME TO SHINE

Holy Spirit, help me to shine bright
Like a shooting star at midnight
So truth will be seen in me;
Help me to live my life holy.

HE PROTECTS YOU WITH HIS SHIELD

You have no reason to fear when Jesus holds a shield
protecting you
From all danger in all directions-- Jesus defeats with His
light and truth.
Storms may stir, but Jesus, Your Savior, will grab the storm
by the horns and cast it down,
Then rush to your rescue, break the shackles binding you,
and place on your head His crown.

MAY I NEVER FORGET

May I never forget that I was lost
Until I met Jesus at the cross
Suffering for all of my sins;
He loved me through thick and thin
With mercy and grace
So I would live by faith.

COMFORT FROM ME

Trust in Me to comfort you
In all the trials you are going through,
I will take you by My hand
To steady your steps and help you stand;
I will give you joy and peace,
I will lift your load to set you free,
All you need is mustard seed faith
And a loving amount of mercy and grace.

YOUR FATHER IS SO LOVING

Your Father is so loving,
He will extend patience for you
To come to the altar
And accept His truth,
He has no desire
For you to be condemned and lost,
Your Father is so loving,
He sent His own Son to the cross.

I NEED YOUR TRUSTING HAND

My Lord, my God, I was troubled and tried to solve this
problem on my own,
But it grieved me even more and only brought me down.
I need Your trusting hand to guide me through this storm
that has blindsided me;
Only You can steady my feet on this rocky road, only You
can set me free.

GODLY POWER

Holy God, only You can break strongholds of the enemy
and rescue the helpless;
Only You have the power to release Satan's grip so the
needy will be blessed;
The Blood of the Lamb has already covered deep wounds
and pain,
And the Holy Spirit guides the hearts of Your obedient
servants who pray for healing rain.

PRAISE ALWAYS

I give thanks always
For a day to give praise
To the Lord of heaven and earth--
Praises upon praises He is worth!

LET US NOT BE BLIND

My Lord, my God, let not Your children be blind
To the writing on the wall and the signs
That You are coming soon--
Only You will rescue us from doom.

JESUS STANDS WAITING

Jesus stands waiting at the door to come in
Your life to lead you away from sin,
He is a patient Savior willing to wait;
You must make a decision before it is too late.

Jesus has already been nailed to the cross
In your place so you would not be lost,
He sacrificed His life and died in your place,
Freely providing you mercy and grace.

Jesus stands waiting-- why not let Him in
And give up your miserable life of sin?
How sad it will be if you wait too late
Then find yourself locked inside Hell's gate.

HANDING YOU OVER TO MY LOVING FATHER

As long as I know our God is a Father Who cares,
I will never give up keeping you in my prayers;
I may not give a call or send a note of love to you,
But I can petition my Lord to send your blessing through.

THANK YOU FOR SALVATION

Jesus, thank You for salvation today
And answering when You heard me pray;
You reached out to me with mercy and grace
As You shined Your light in my face.

ANSWERED PRAYER

Pray and keep believing
A blessing you will be receiving
When God's heart is touched
Because He loves you so much.

His Word is light and truth
Producing the breakthrough
When you plant the seed
Into your need.

Patience works with faith
As God's mercy and grace
Brings forth fruit
Straight from the root.

THANK YOU FOR BLESSING US

Thank You, my Father, for blessing us beyond what we
deserve;
Your kind heart generously overflows with love, and You
keep Your Word.
Guide me to give with an open heart, to love freely, and to
reach out to those in need
As I live to give You glory while sowing seeds.

PREPARATION

The Lord is handling your prayer
With tender mercy and care
While preparing your heart during the wait;
He is never too soon or too late.

HELP ME TO DO RIGHT

My dear Father, impart in me to willingly obey all of your
commands,
And to freely offer a loving heart and helping hands
To all kinds of needs as I live in Your light;
Most of all help me to do right.

THE KEY

In my Savior's hands I place
All of my hope-- His saving grace
Is the key to every locked door;
I can ask for nothing more.

YOUR LOVE IS AWESOME

My Father, Your love is so awesome, I cannot comprehend
Why I deserve the many blessings You bestow upon me;
I offer everything within me to send
To You praises, honor, thanksgiving, and glory.

HEAL US ALL

Spirit of the Holy Living God, I pray healing to all,
Young and old, rich and poor, big and small;
Bind wounds and mend hearts that are broken,
Restore relationships and soothe feelings by harsh words
spoken;
Spirit of the Holy Living God, return peace to broken
homes and make them again whole;
Most of all, change all hearts and save every soul.

YOU BLESS US WITH PERFECT PEACE

Thank You, Jesus, my Savior, for Your willingness
To answer prayer as You bless
Us with Your perfect peace;
You meet all of our needs.

MORE THAN ENOUGH

God's love is more than enough
To supply the needs of all of us;
He is willing to give with a free hand
Faith and strength to help us stand.

OPEN THE DOOR

My Holy Father, my heart longs
To be in Your house singing praise songs,
Fellowshipping with family and friends,
And worshiping, hoping it never ends.

How I would love the wine and bread
To remember how my Savior was broken and bled
On that old rugged cross
So my soul would not be lost.

I pray You make a way
We can again walk up and pray
At the altar as we did before--
Oh, my dear Lord, open the door!

A BEAUTIFUL GLORIOUS DAY

This old earth will fade away
One beautiful, glorious day,
And heaven will also be new,
Glorious all the way through and through.
New Jerusalem will come down
Upon the new earth as a holy crown,
And our Lord will live among His people
Worshiping without a building with a steeple.

KEEPING YOU IN PRAYER

I will tenderly love and care
As I keep you in prayer,
Lifting you in God's grace
For His light to shine on your face.

KEEP THE FAITH

Keep the faith,
Watch and wait,
Jesus, our King soon will be
Coming in His glory
To gather us in His hand
For the Promised Land.

THANK YOU FOR KEEPING YOUR WORD

Thank You, my Lord, for keeping Your Word which renews
and restores my faith;
I believe Your report for You have never let me down-- You
always do as You say.
Whenever darkness comes and I lose my footing during the
night,
I know in the morning You will awaken the sun and bring
forth light.

A MEASURE OF FAITH

The Father lovingly cares
As He answers prayers
Never too soon or too late
And always with a measure of faith.

JESUS SACRIFICED HIS LIFE

If Jesus sacrificed His life on the cross
And rose alive so all of our sins would be forgiven,
Then we would have no reason to be lost,
And every life would be worth living--

From all feeble old men and old ladies
To the disabled and the unborn babies,
There is no reason to hate the neighbors we meet
And no reason for unrest in the cities and violence in the
streets.

If Jesus sacrificed His life and returned to heaven above,
Then we should reach out in love to each other
As we receive joy and peace while living in His love--
Together we are all sisters and brothers.

A LOVING HEART

Love does not overpower with knowledge,
It helps with a heart lowly and humble;
Love lifts with caring hands
And causes no one to stumble.

TO HONOR YOU

Jesus, I long to honor You
In all I do
With a heart filled with praise;
Guide me in Your ways.

WHY I FORMED YOU

I formed you in My likeness,
Perfect, flawless, and blessed
To enjoy the love and peace I give
While you abundantly live.

LOVE NEVER ENDS

Love never ends,
Love attends and mends
Pain and sorrow
And brings a beautiful tomorrow.

YOUR GIFT OF LIFE

Thank You, Holy Father, for the life You give
So we will truly live
For Your kingdom and glory;
Your gift of life is holy.

PROTECT YOUR CHILDREN

Almighty Lord, God, our Father, You are in control
Of the waves and wind as well as souls;
Please gather the coming storms inside Your wings
And provide Your children protective surroundings.

STURDY AND STRONG

Trust Me when you are too weak to stand,
Sturdy and strong is My hand;
I will lift you to higher heights
And restore and increase your appetite.

COMFORT MY NEIGHBOR

My Lord, comfort my neighbor in Your arms
And protect him from further harm;
Guide him with Your light
To a future shining bright.

GOD'S LOVE NEVER ENDS

God's love never ends
As He opens His heart and sends
Blessings as rain from the sky
And hope as an eagle flying high.

WE PLACE OUR FAITH IN YOU

My Lord, protect us with Your trusting hand
As we journey through troubled land;
We place all of our faith in You
To guide us through and through.

WHAT TRUTH DOES

Truth removes the veil covering the face
So God's glory, mercy, and grace
Will penetrate the mind
Of humankind.

OPEN OUR EYES

Jesus, open our eyes to Your saving grace
And turn us away from evil ways;
Sin has blinded our minds to Your truth,
And we are no longer seeking You.

Words From Benita Nichols

As a Southern lady from Alabama, I am a lover of nature where I can discern the fingerprints of God Almighty. I express my love for Jesus, my Savior, in books of inspirational poetry I have published, I enjoyed having stories and rhymes read to me when I was a small child and developed a love for reading when I was in elementary school.

I was a little girl who enjoyed role playing with my dolls which I had named and given voices to. As I grew, I began writing poetry and stories. Beginning in my late teens, I developed characters which are found in the series of plays I have written.